PIANO CLASSICS

T0040883

CONTENTS

ISBN 978-0-7935-0244-8

HAL•LEONARD®
CORPORATION
7777 W. BLUEMOUND RD. P.O. BOX 13819 MILWAUKEE, WI 53213

JOE RAPOSO

JOE RAPOSO's musical accomplishments blanket a territory from Sesame Street, to the stages of Broadway and Moscow. As musical director and one of the creators of Sesame Street, he's written award-winning songs for Kermit The Frog and the entire Sesame Street gang. He won an Oscar nomination for his score to The Great Muppet Caper, and has earned five Grammy's along with many gold and platinum records.

Joe Raposo has written music for a myriad of top stars like Frank Sinatra, Barbra Streisand, Ray Charles, and Woody Allen. His award-winning songs include Sing, It's Not Easy Bein' Green, Here's To The Winners, and You Will Be My Music. He's been associated with many award-winning television specials, and the Boston Pops Orchestra recorded an entire album of his music.

In 1986, Joe composed the score for Raggedy Ann. This musical was chosen by the U.S. State Department and the Soviet Government to be the first cultural exchange with the Soviet Union in 10 years. The show opened in Moscow with critical and popular success prior to Broadway.

Joe studied music at Harvard University and in Paris as a pupil of Nadia Boulanger, legendary mentor of George Gershwin, Aaron Copeland, and Leonard Bernstein.

Joe is a director of The Third Street Music School in New York City. Here Joe shares his love of music by teaching others the joy of learning to play. Teaching music is not new to the Raposo family. Joe's father, a noted violinist now retired, was a renowned and innovative teacher, especially for the beginning player.

"I designed EASY ADULT PIANO for the amateur pianist," says Joe. "With this easy to read and play notation system, even the novice can discover quickly and easily how anyone can progress rapidly while enjoying the fantastic experience of playing great music."

Joe Raposo with Mrs. Reagan and lyricist Hal David at the audition of their song for Mrs. Reagan's To Love A Child campaign.

Joe and some of his gang from the Third Street Music School.

THE NEW YORK STATE MUSIC AWARD
1982
presented to

Joe Raposo

His contribution to American song is distinguished by the hallmarks of sincerity and true sentiment. His music for the Public Television series "Sesame Street" and his songs for the great singers of our age have established him as musical spokesman for our generation, whose language reminds each of us that compassion and caring make a better world.

Plaque citing Joe Raposo as recipient of the New York State Music Award, 1982.

THINGS TO KNOW ABOUT
EASY ADULT PIANO MUSIC

Here are some things which will make your piano playing easier and more fun.

Notes That Name Themselves

Easy Adult Piano music is written on a double staff. The upper staff is the **treble** (𝄞) staff and contains the melody usually played by your right hand. The lower **bass** (𝄢) staff contains the accompaniment part and is played by your left hand.

The lower bass staff in Easy Adult Piano has a unique feature to help make your playing easier. There are letters in the notes. If you're not used to reading bass notes, the letters will help you learn faster and play better (and it saves you the time of writing them in, which we know a lot of you do).

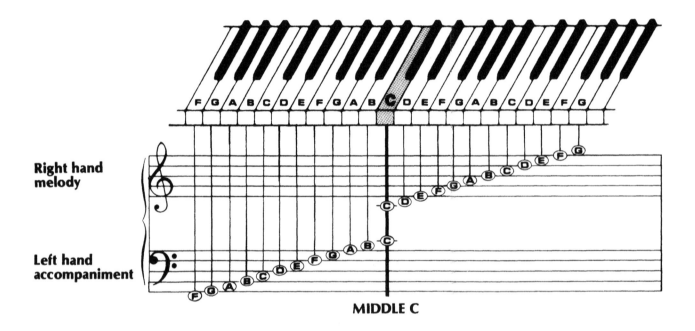

Right hand melody

Left hand accompaniment

MIDDLE C

Note Values

In music, time is measured in **beats**. The illustration shows the types of notes you'll play and how many beats each type receives.

Rests are shown in the lower part of the illustration, along with the number of beats each type receives. A **rest** indicates a period of silence—when you don't play. Rests are still counted, however.

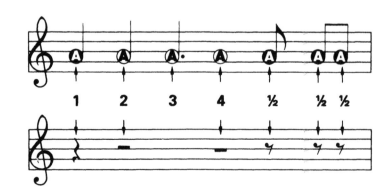

Playing The Black Keys

To make your playing easier, **sharps** (♯) or **flats** (♭) are placed in front of all notes to be played on black keys. A **natural** (♮) is used occasionally to cancel the effect of a previous sharp or flat.

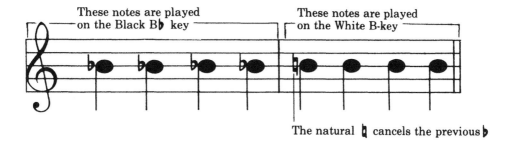

These notes are played on the Black B♭ key

These notes are played on the White B-key

The natural ♮ cancels the previous ♭

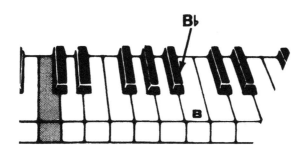

B♭

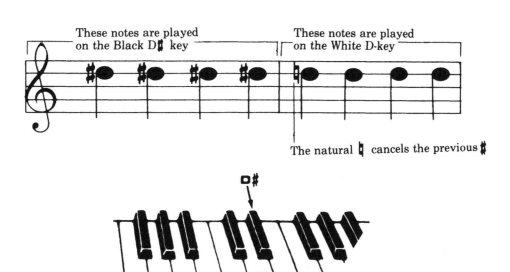

These notes are played on the Black D♯ key

These notes are played on the White D-key

The natural ♮ cancels the previous ♯

D♯

6

Chord Symbols

Small **chord symbols** appear above your music. If your instrument is an electronic keyboard with an automatic chord feature, use the chord symbols to accompany the melody rather than the left-hand part indicated by the **bass clef** (𝄢). Refer to your instrument's Owner's Manual for details on automatic chords.

In the case you know something about harmony, you can also use the chord symbols as a guide in creating your own pianistic "touches" to each arrangement.

CLAIRE DE LUNE

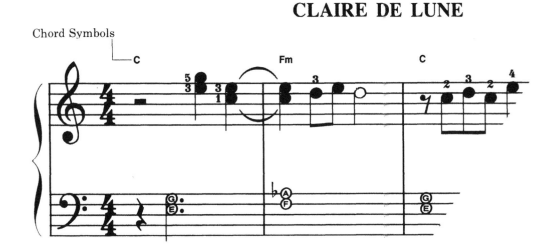

Fingering

Small numbers appear near some of the notes. These are finger numbers and they'll help you play more smoothly. They correspond to your fingers as shown. If you use the finger numbers to play the indicated notes, you'll find playing a lot easier. If, while you're playing, you find a fingering style you like better, use it.

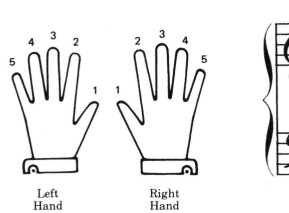

Left
Hand

Right
Hand

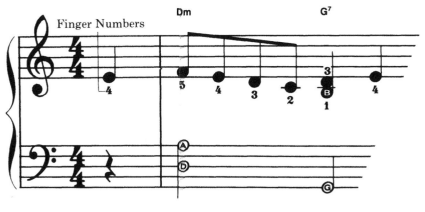

Pedaling Symbols

Occasionally, use of the **sustain pedal** is indicated by these symbols. Press, hold, and release the pedal as indicated in the illustration below.

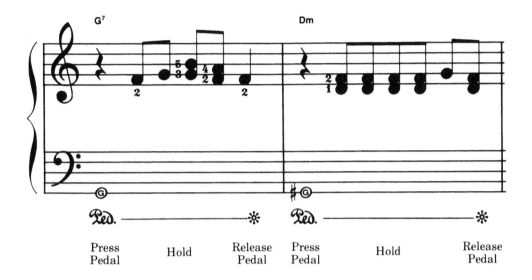

| Press Pedal | Hold | Release Pedal | Press Pedal | Hold | Release Pedal |

8va

This is an **octave** sign. It appears above or below certain groups of notes to indicate they should be played an octave (8 white keys) higher than written. **8 basso** indicates notes which are to be played an octave lower than written.

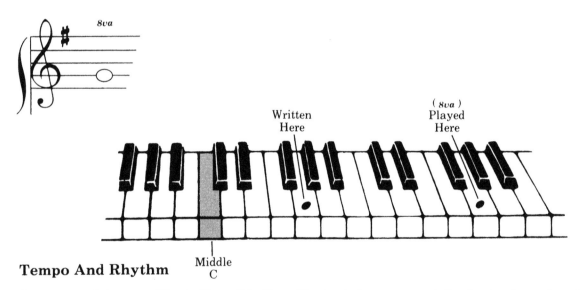

Tempo And Rhythm

A suggested **tempo** (Fast, Slow, Medium Fast, etc.) appears at the beginning of each Easy Adult Piano arrangement. Use this as a guide to how fast or slow you should be playing.

Along with the tempo, in most cases, is a **rhythm** name (SWING, WALTZ, etc.) This is also a guide to the rhythmic "feel" the arrangement should have.

If you have an electronic keyboard with automatic rhythm, use the suggested tempo and rhythm as a guide to setting the controls for this feature.

CLAIRE DE LUNE

CLAUDE DEBUSSY
Arranged by
JOE RAPOSO

Slow

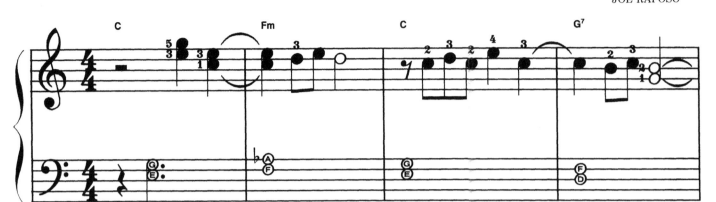

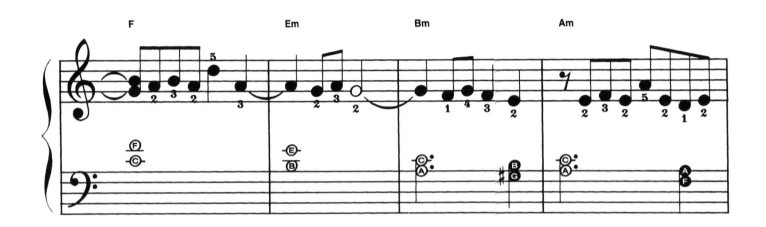

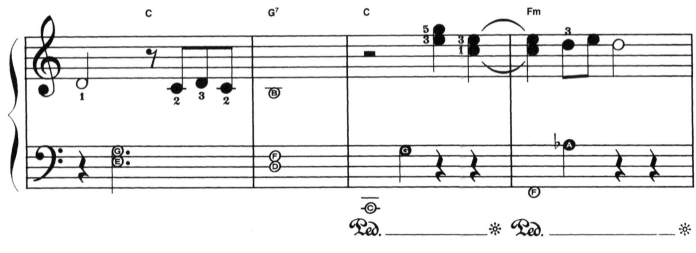

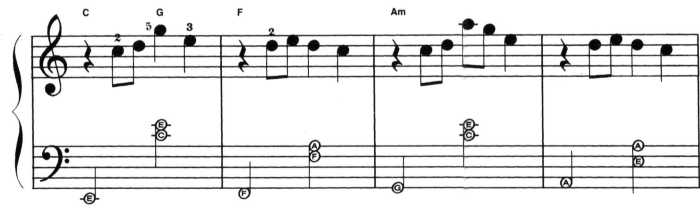

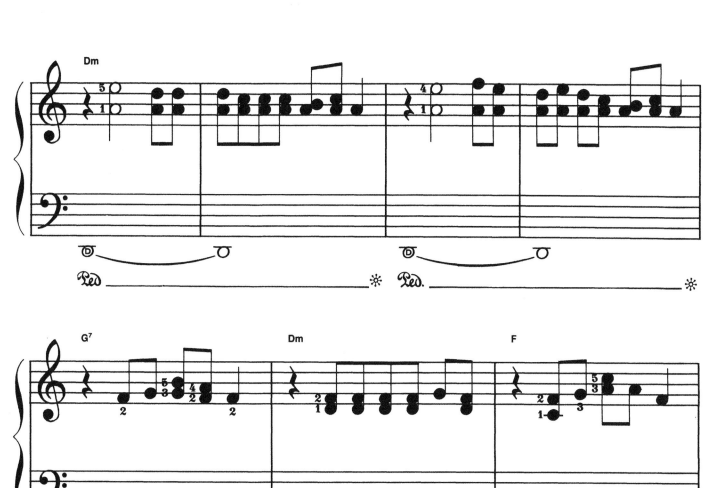

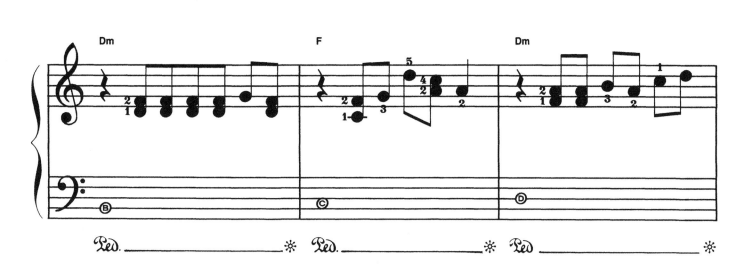

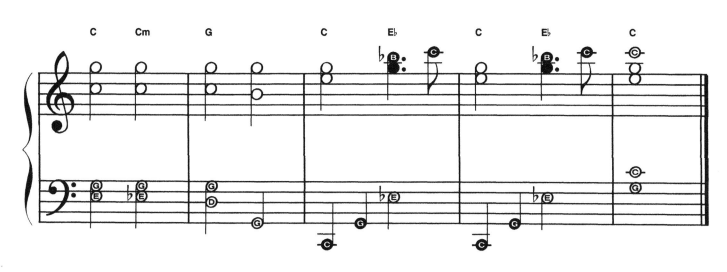

ELEGY

JULES M. MASSENET
Arranged by
JOE RAPOSO

Slow

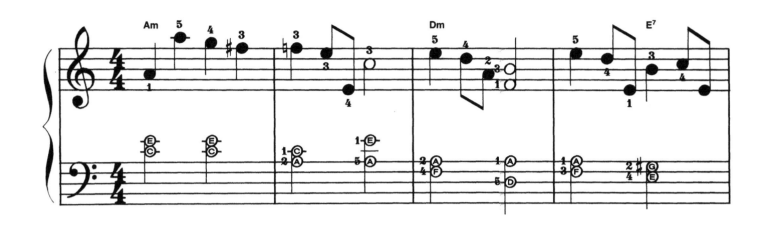

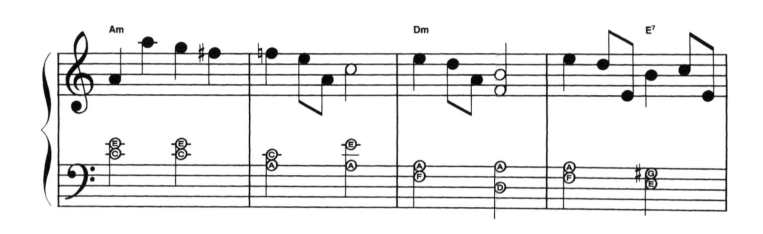

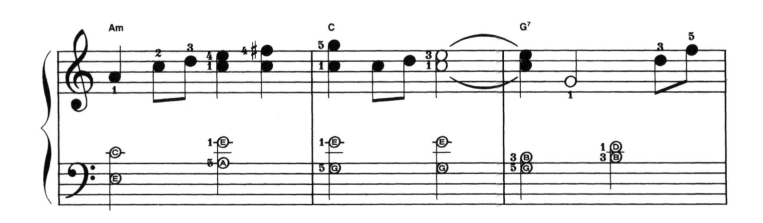

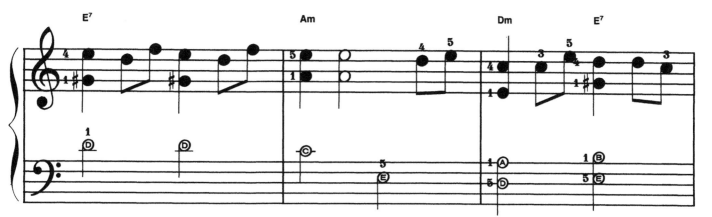

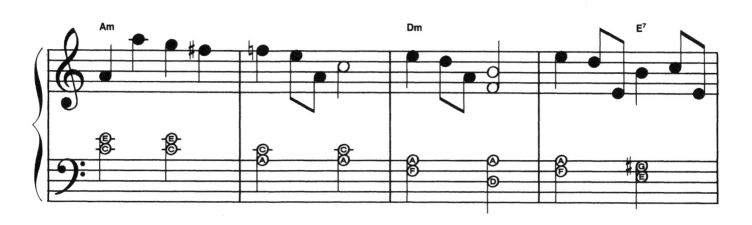

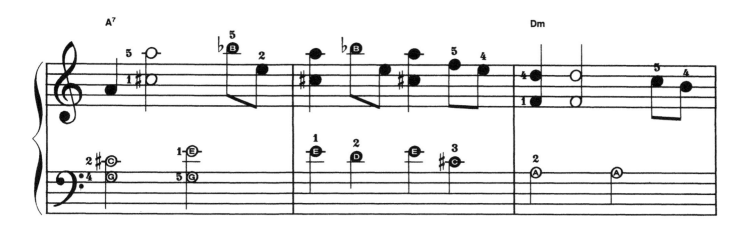

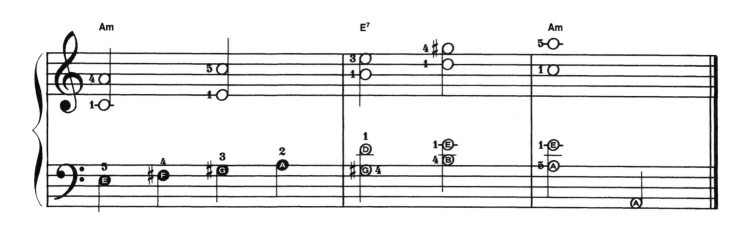

ETUDE

FREDERIC CHOPIN

Arranged by
JOE RAPOSO

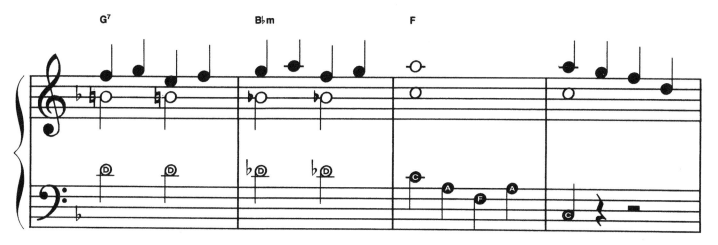

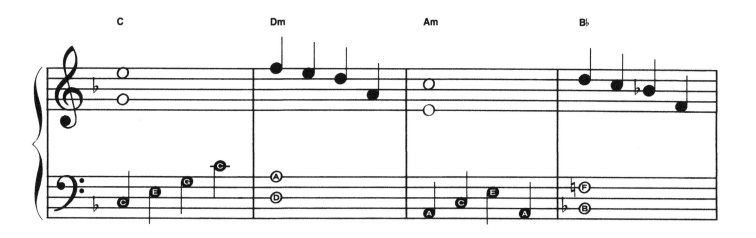

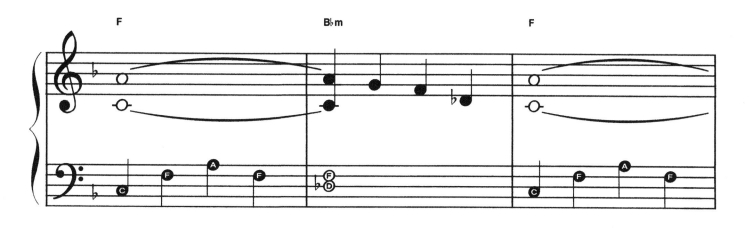

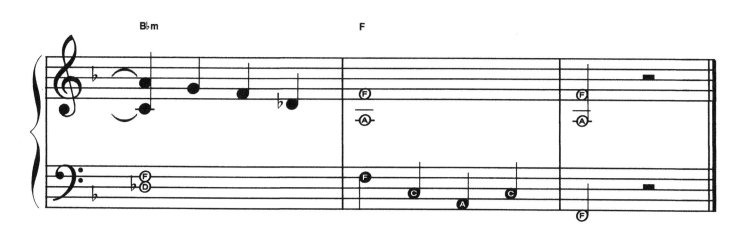

FANTASIE IMPROMPTU
(I'm Always Chasing Rainbows)

FREDERIC CHOPIN

Arranged by
JOE RAPOSO

Slow

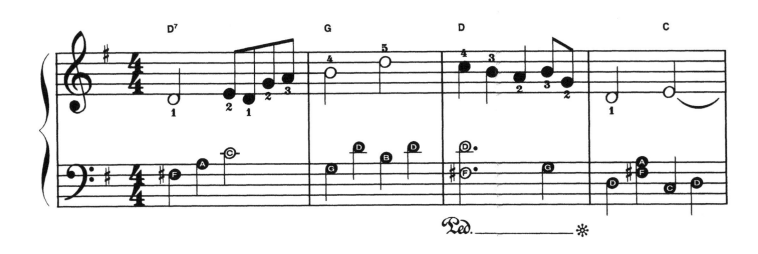

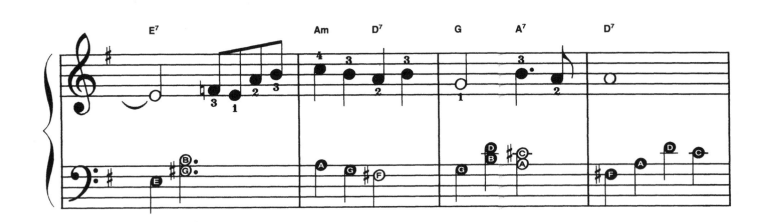

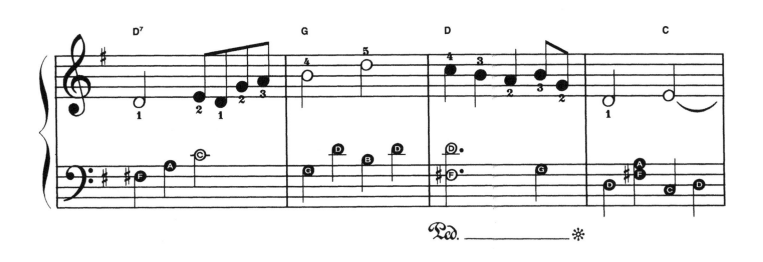

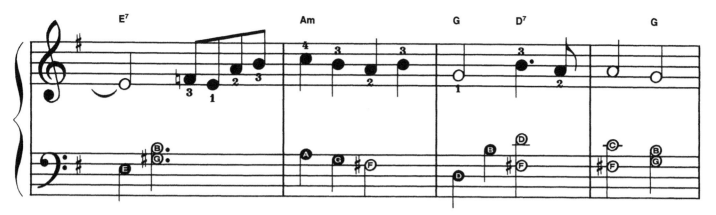

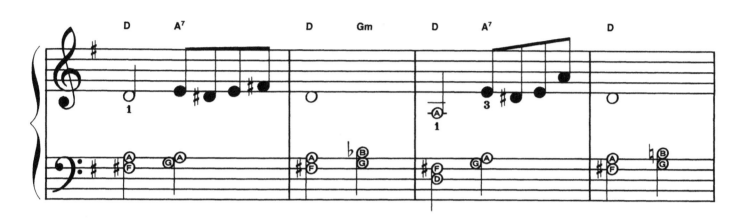

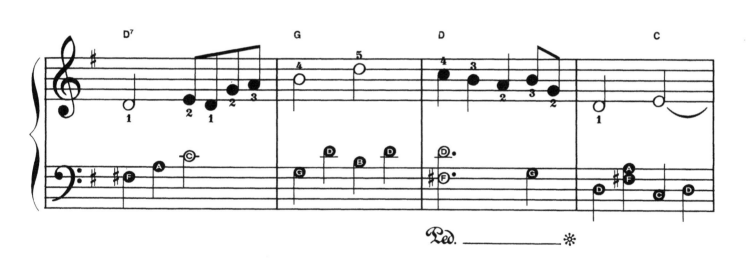

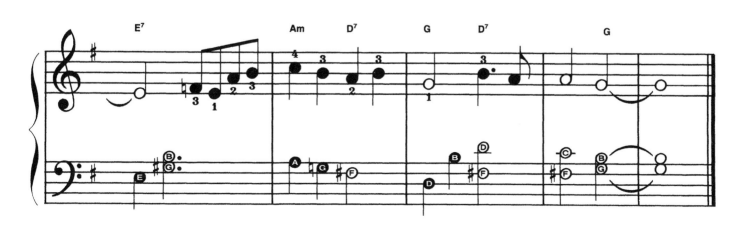

FÜR ELISE

LUDWIG VAN BEETHOVEN
Arranged by
JOE RAPOSO

Medium

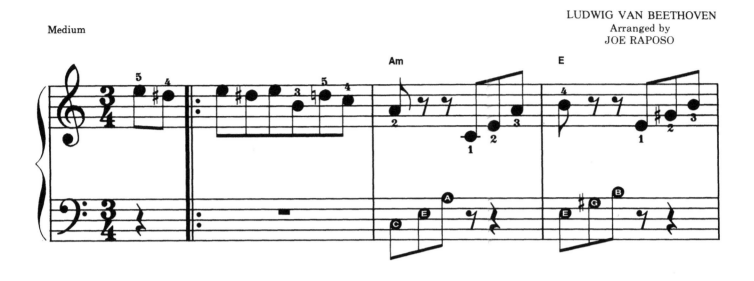

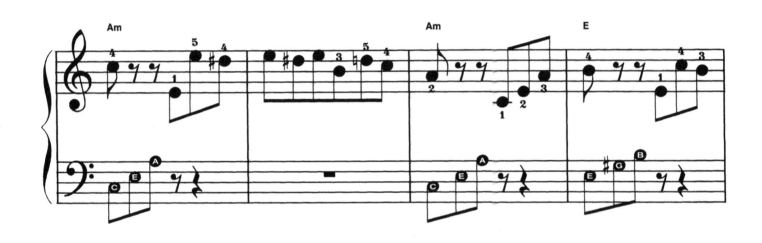

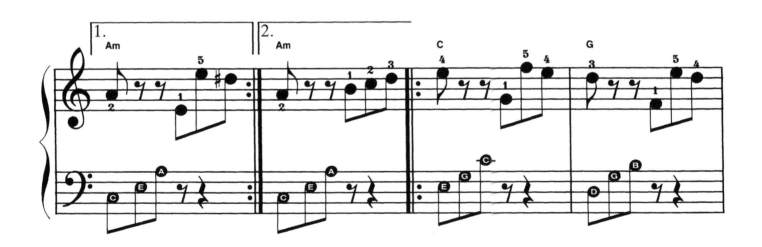

THE HAPPY FARMER

ROBERT SCHUMANN

Arranged by
JOE RAPOSO

Medium Fast

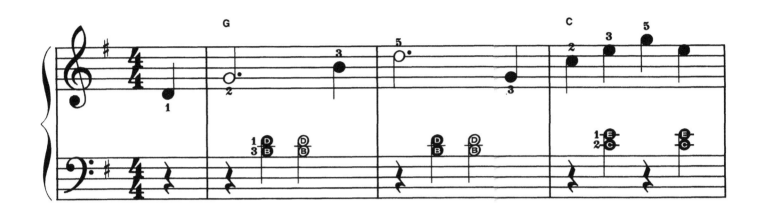

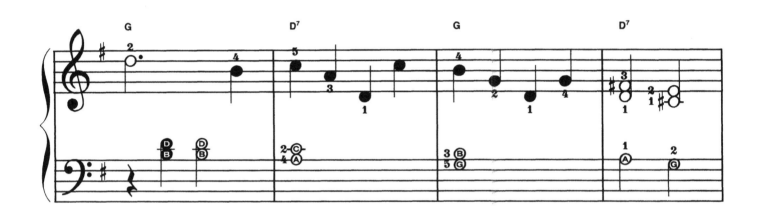

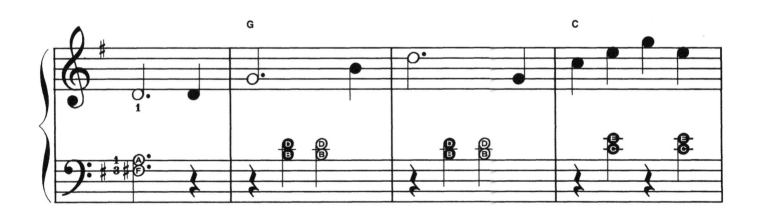

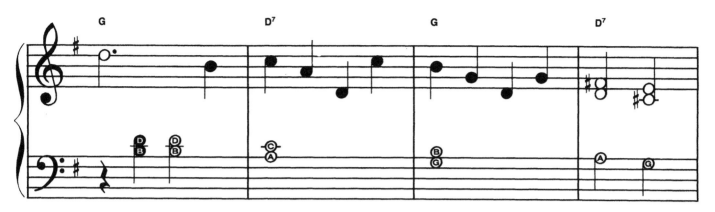

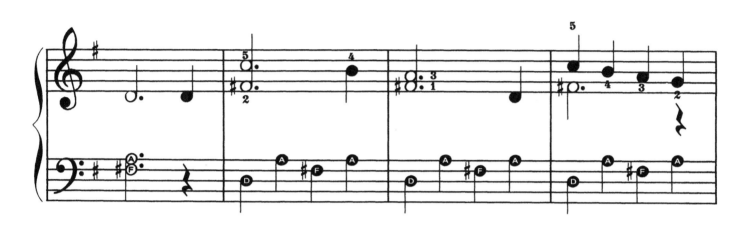

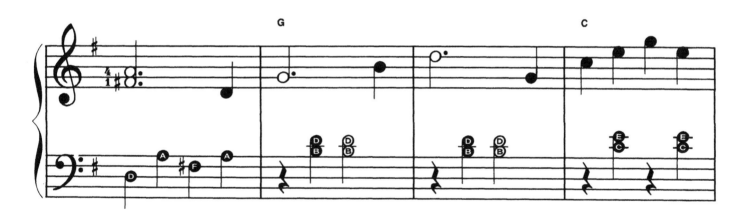

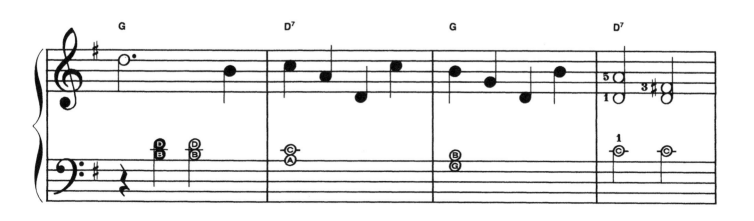

20

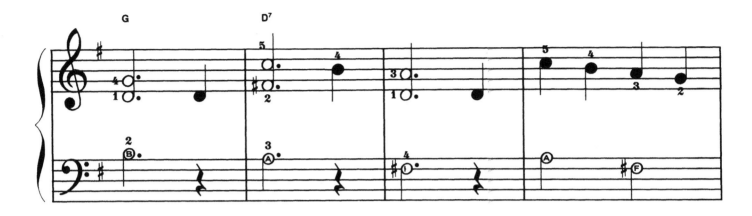

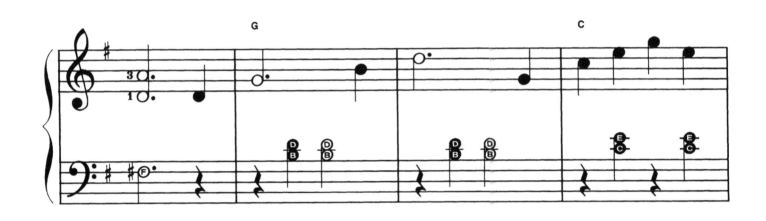

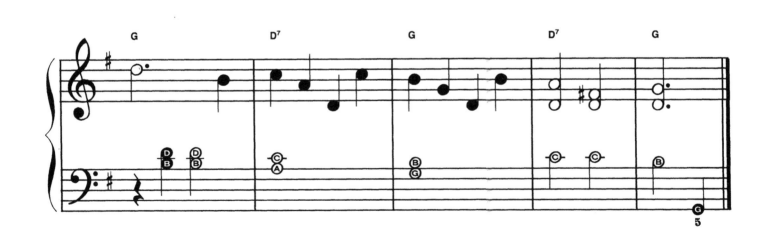

LIEBESTRAUM

FRANZ LISZT
Arranged by
JOE RAPOSO

Medium

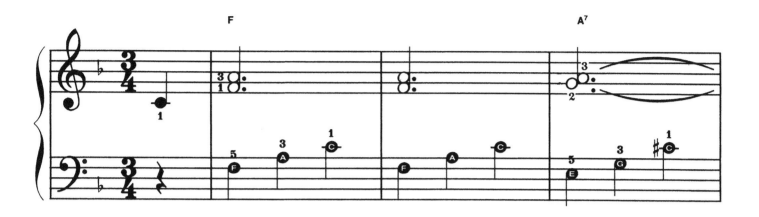

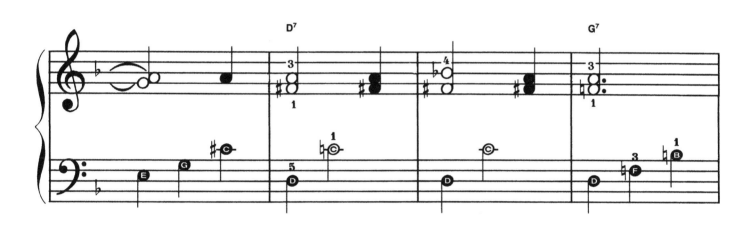

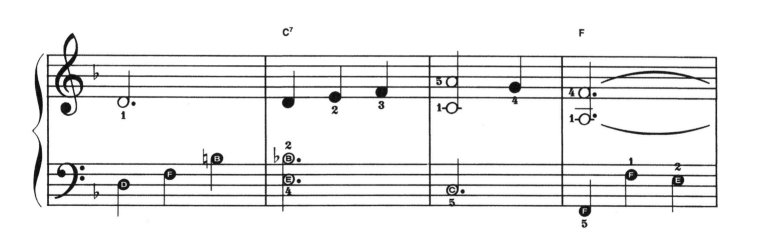

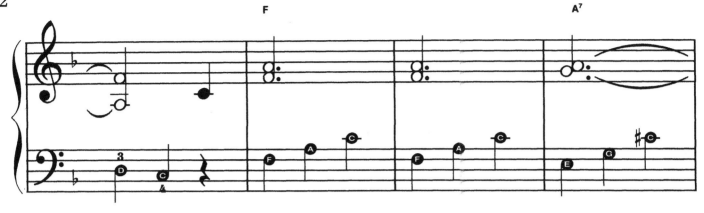

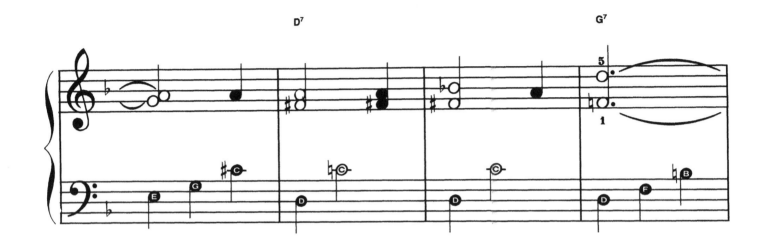

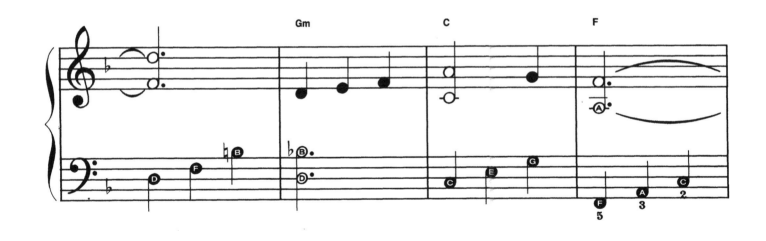

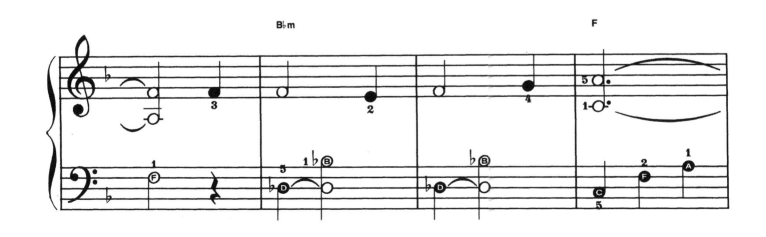

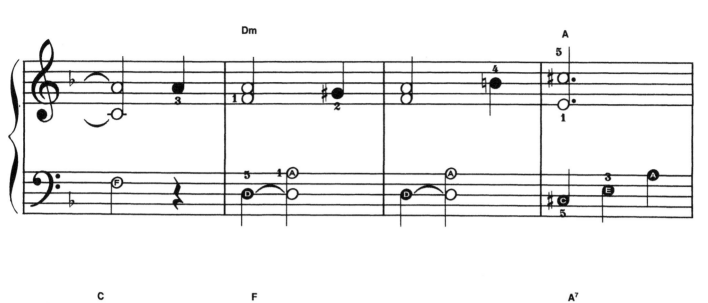

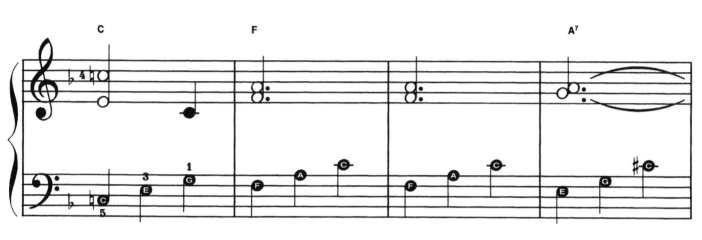

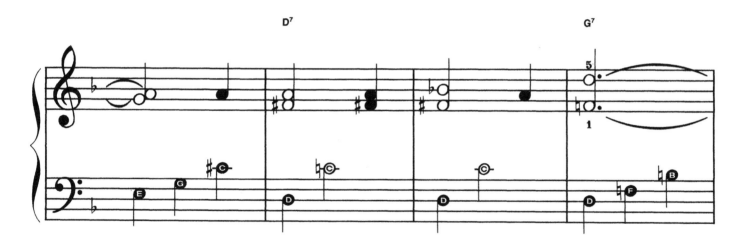

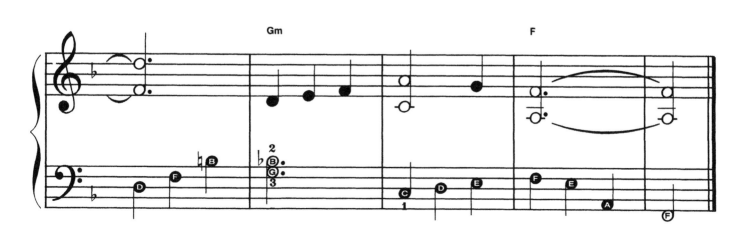

MINUET IN G

LUDWIG VAN BEETHOVEN

Arranged by
JOE RAPOSO

Medium

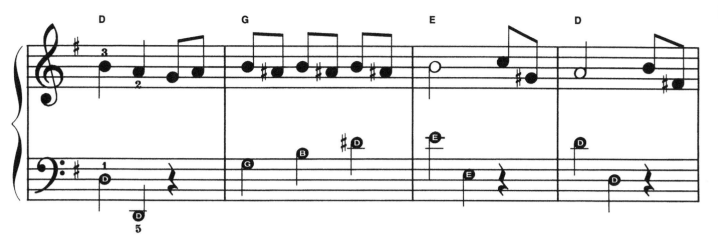

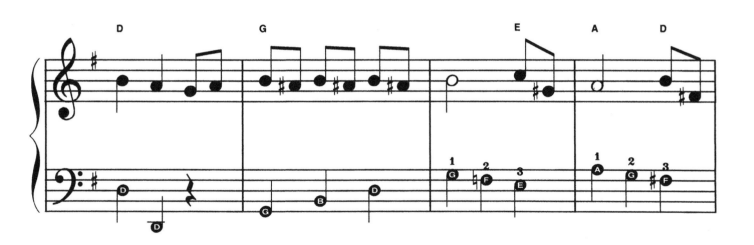

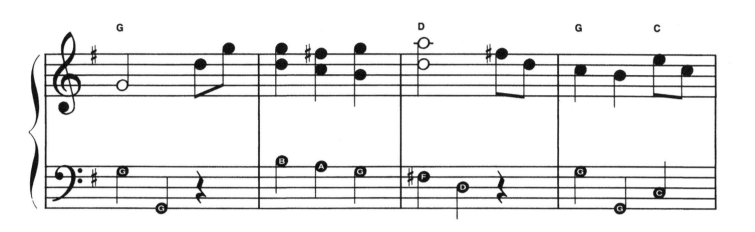

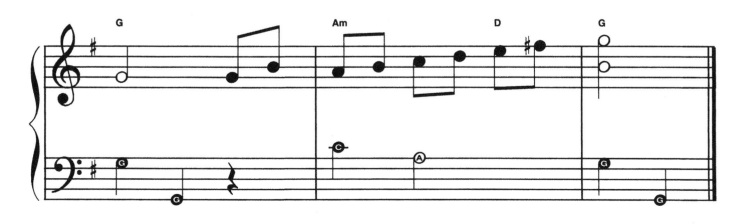

MINUET NO. 1

JOHANN SEBASTIAN BACH
Arranged by
JOE RAPOSO

Medium

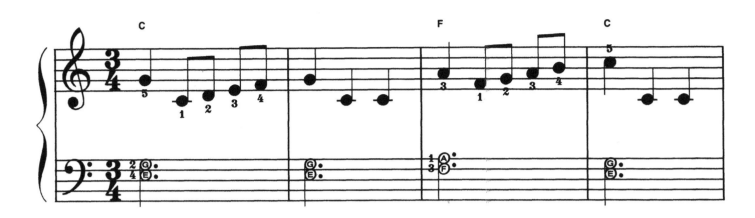

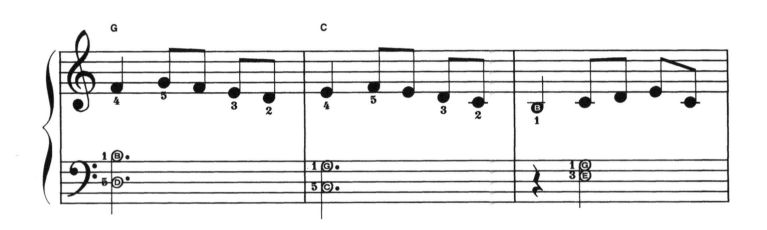

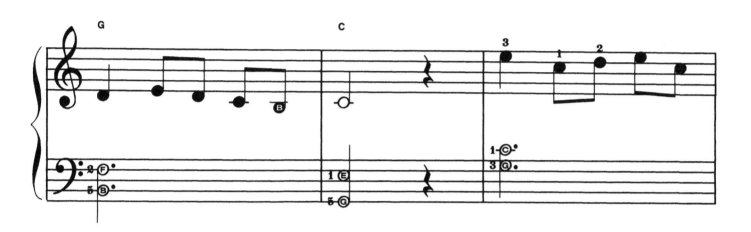

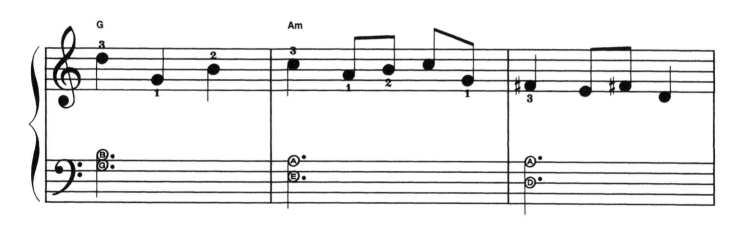

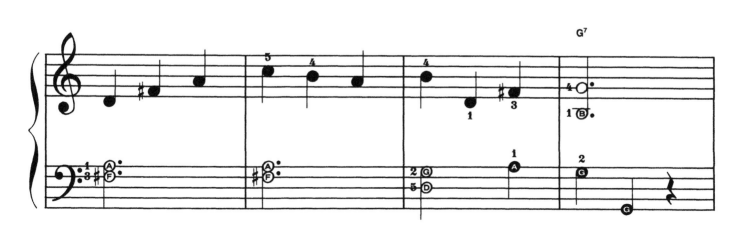

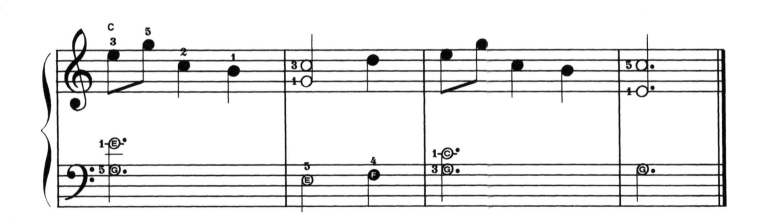

LULLABY

JOHANNES BRAHMS
Arranged by
JOE RAPOSO

Slow

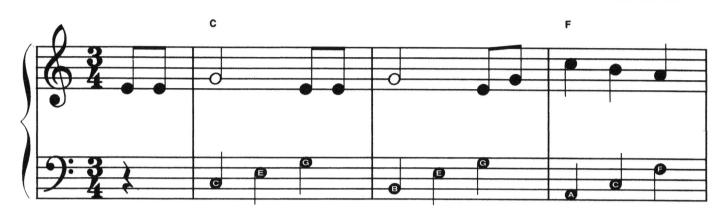

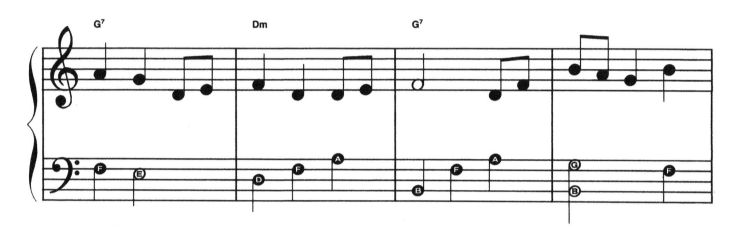

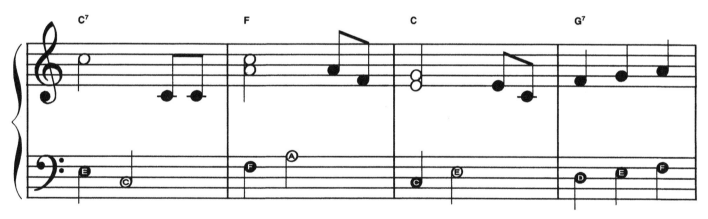

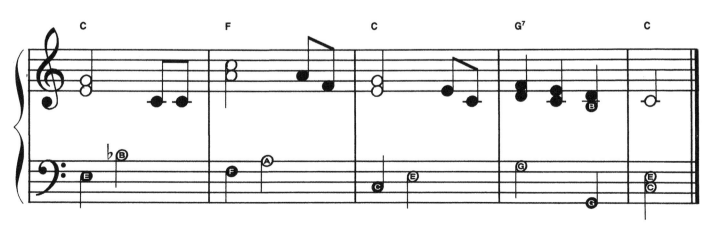

NOCTURNE
(Op. 9 No. 2)

FREDERIC CHOPIN

Arranged by
JOE RAPOSO

Medium Slow

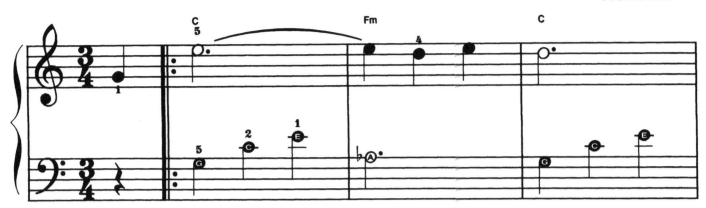

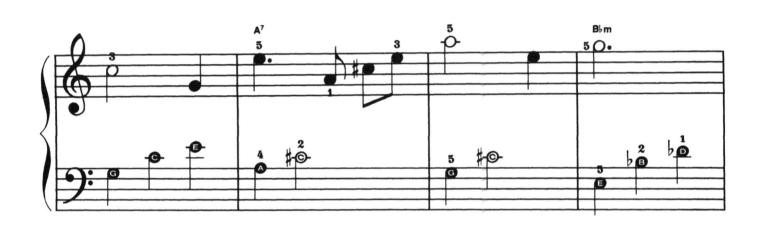

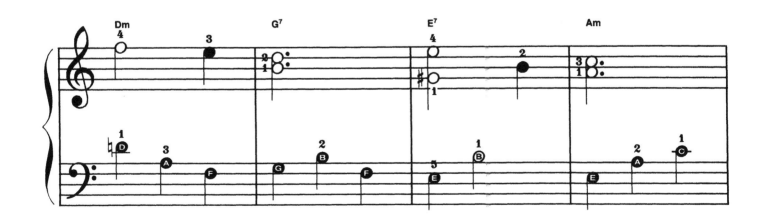

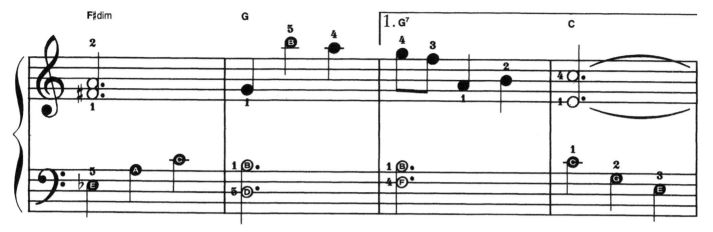

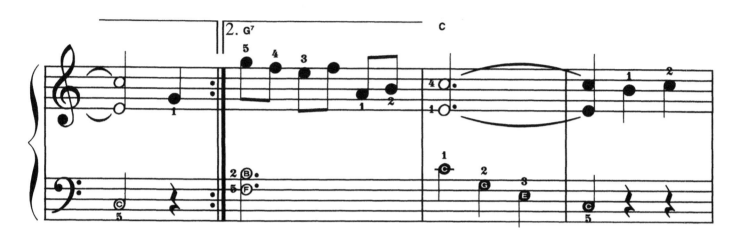

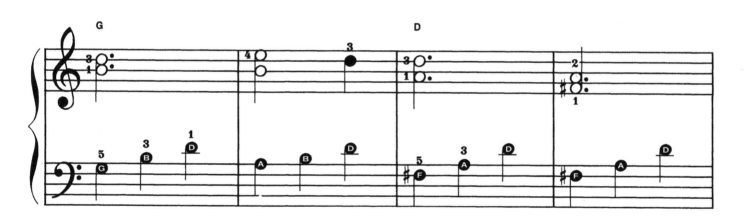

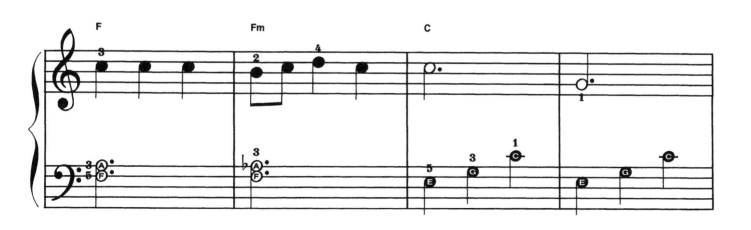

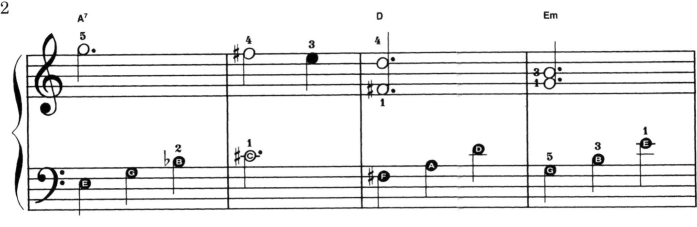

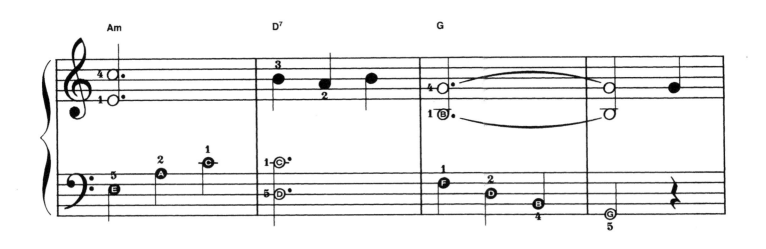

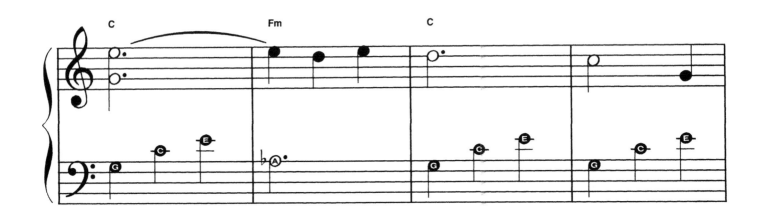

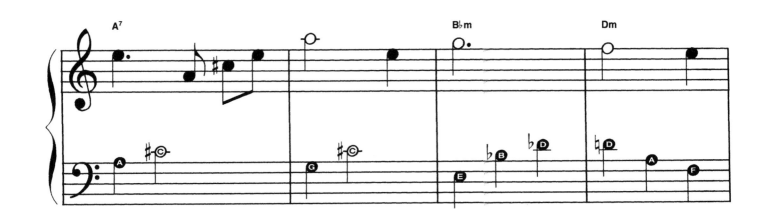

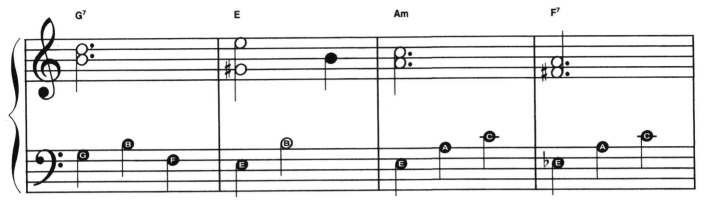

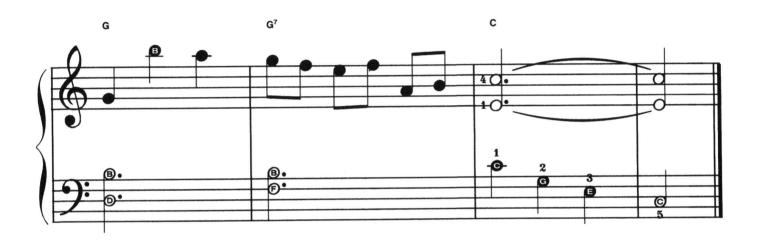

PRELUDE OP. 28 NO. 7

FREDERIC CHOPIN

Arranged by
JOE RAPOSO

Medium

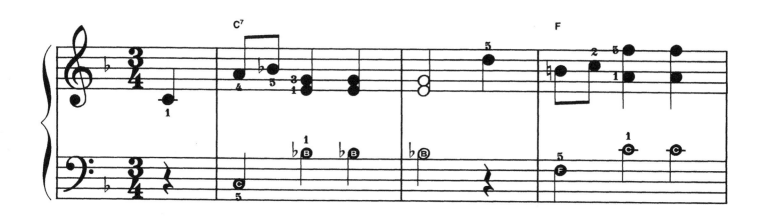

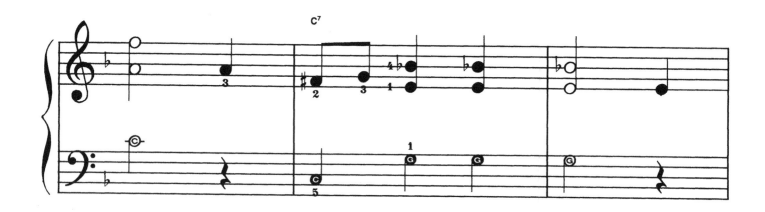

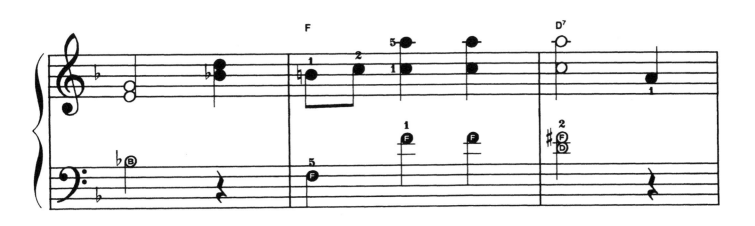

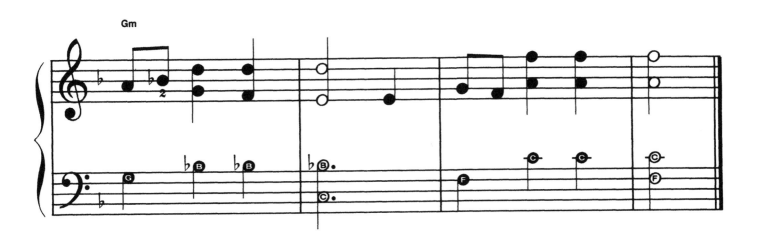

POLOVETZIAN DANCE

ALEXANDER BORODIN

Arranged by
JOE RAPOSO

Slow

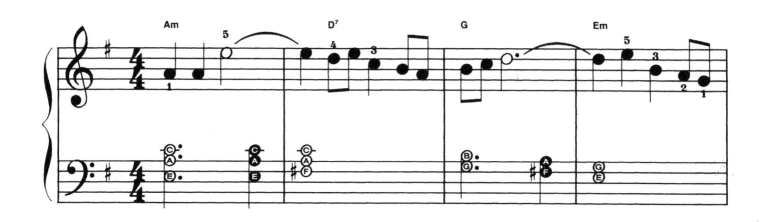

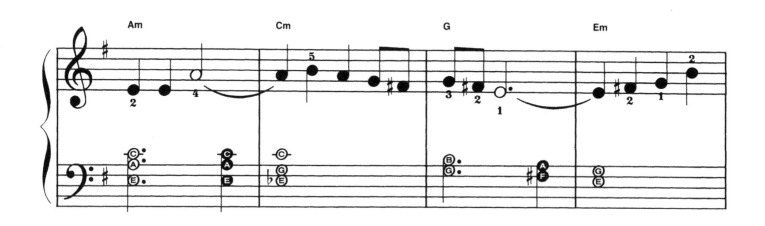

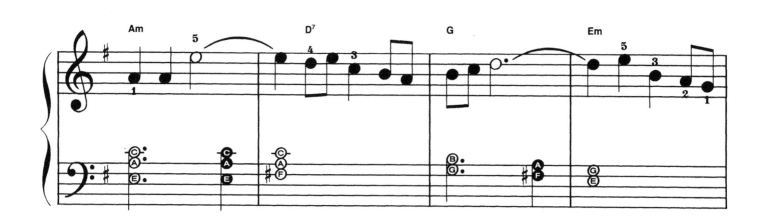

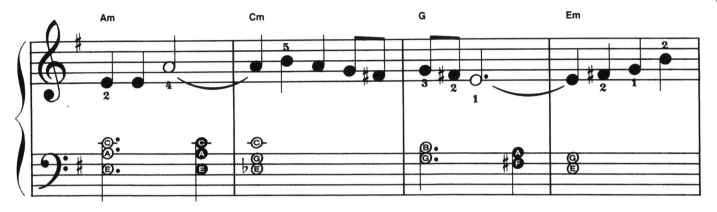

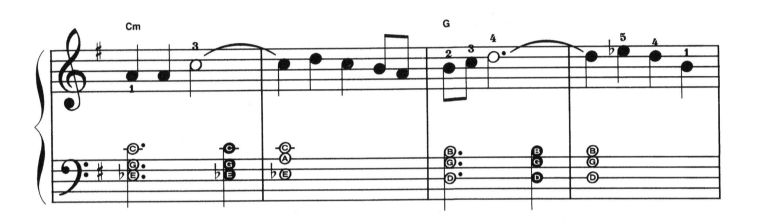

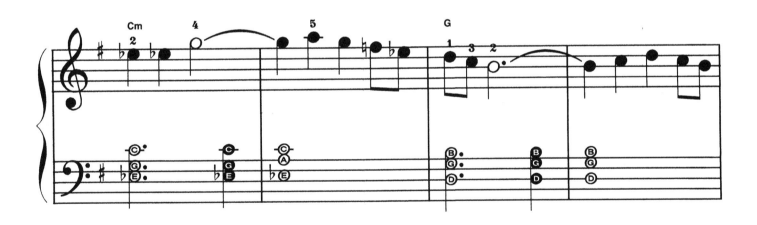

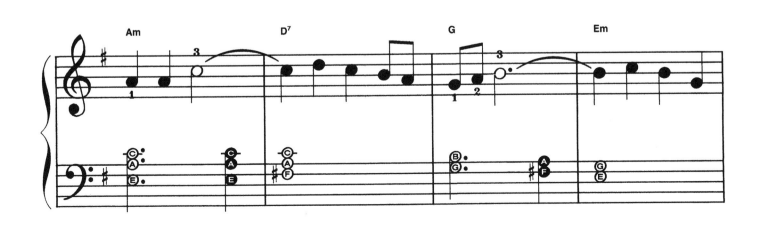

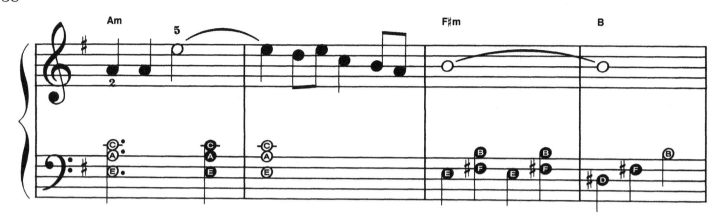

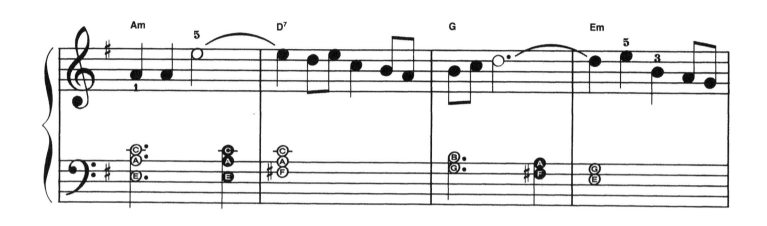

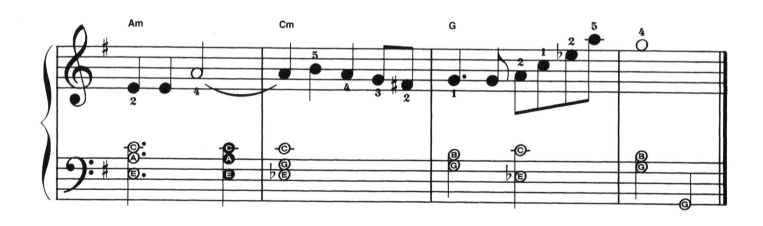

TRÄUMEREI

ROBERT A. SCHUMANN
Arranged by
JOE RAPOSO

Medium Slow

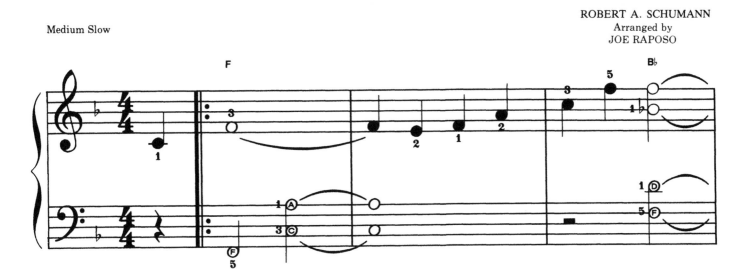

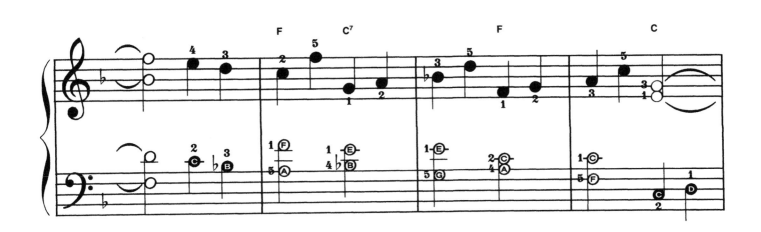

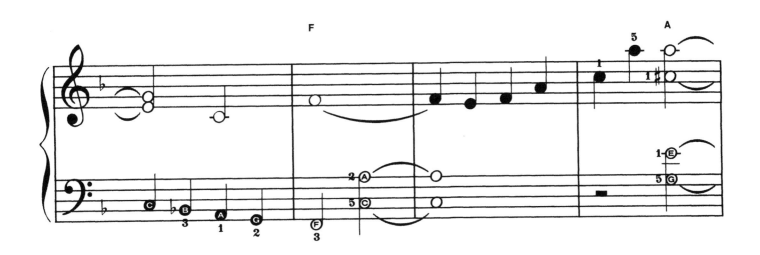

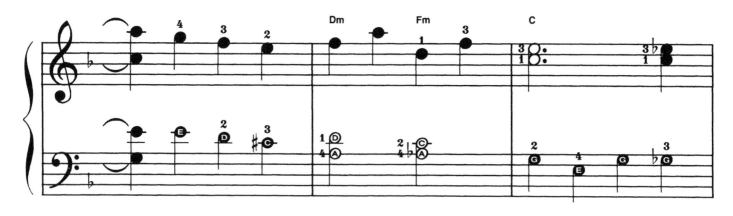

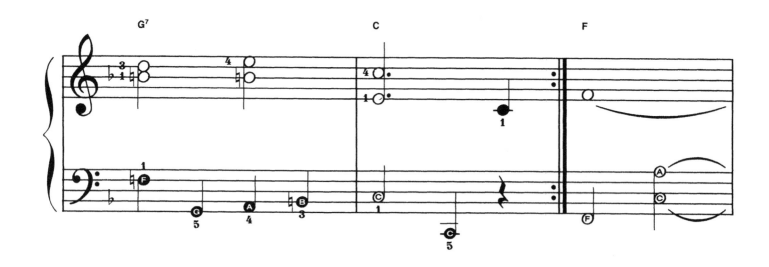

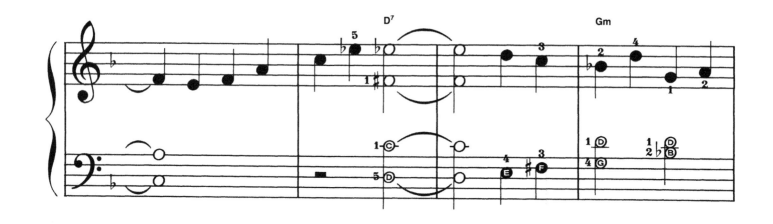

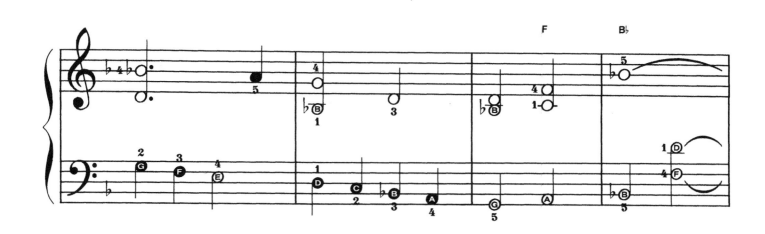

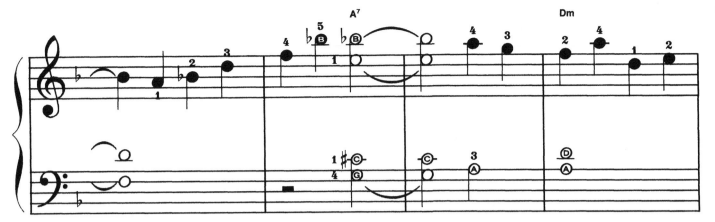

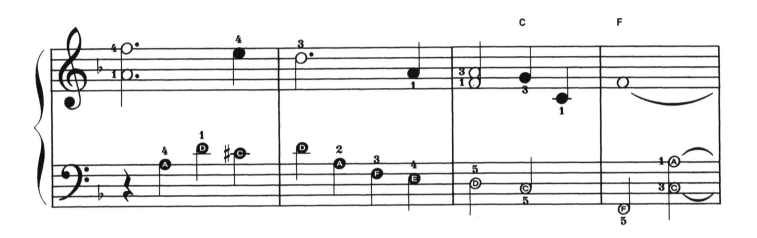

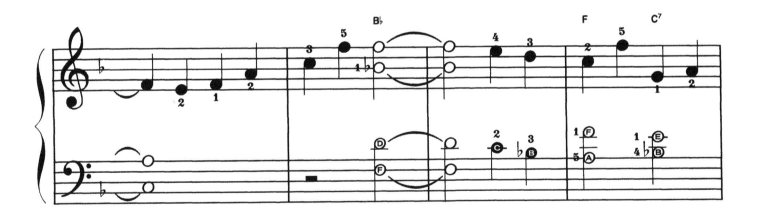

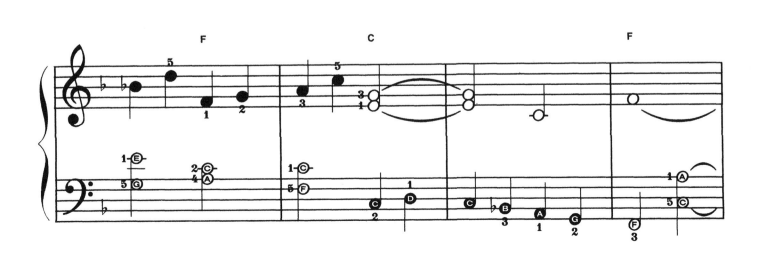

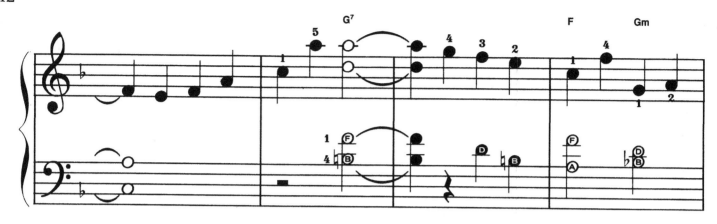

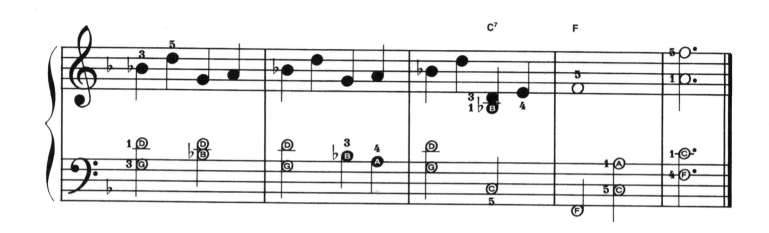

Medium

VALSE

FREDERIC CHOPIN

Arranged by
JOE RAPOSO

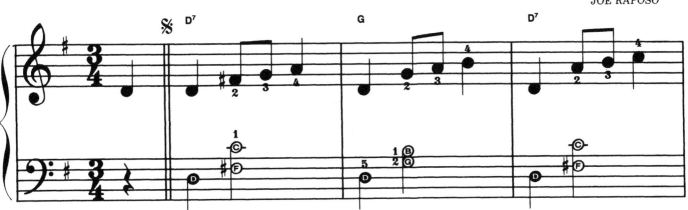

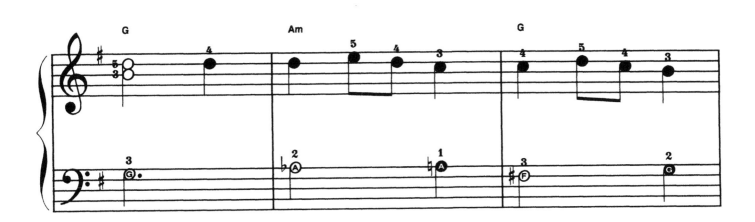

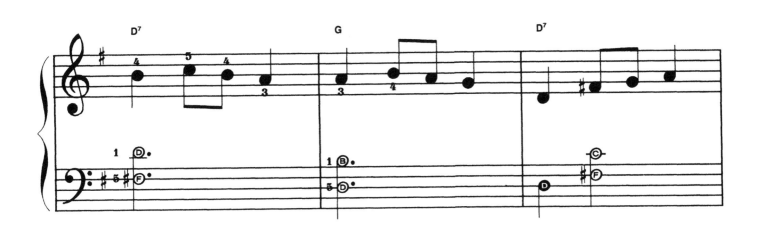

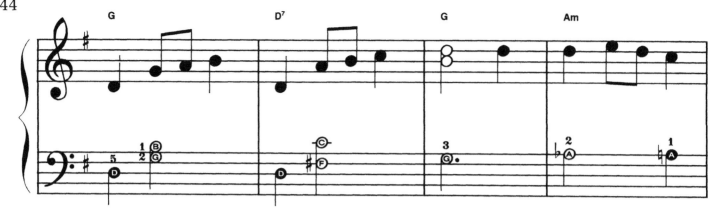

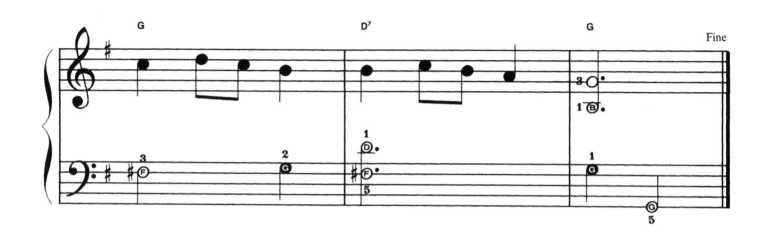

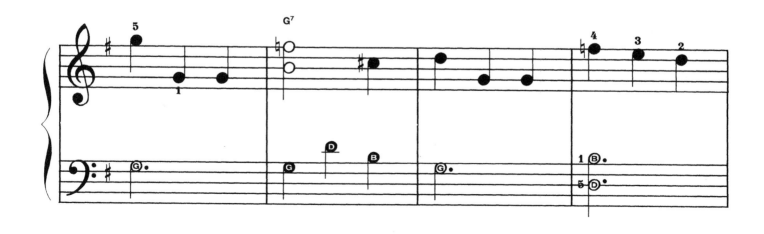

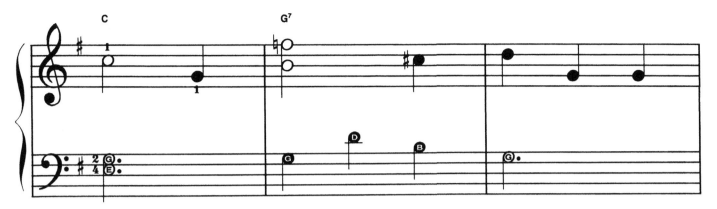

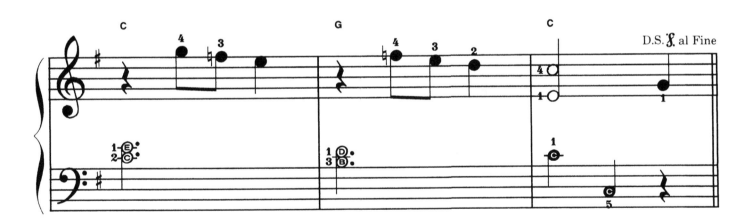

TALES FROM THE VIENNA WOODS

JOHANN STRAUSS
Arranged by
JOE RAPOSO

Medium Fast

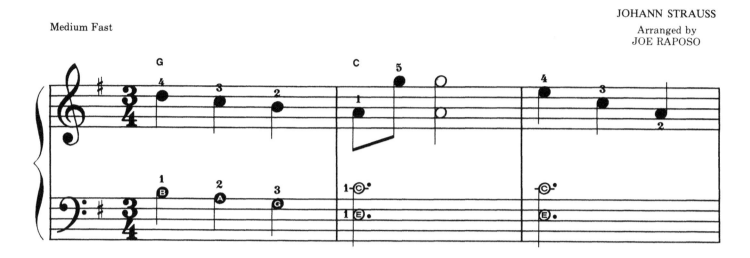

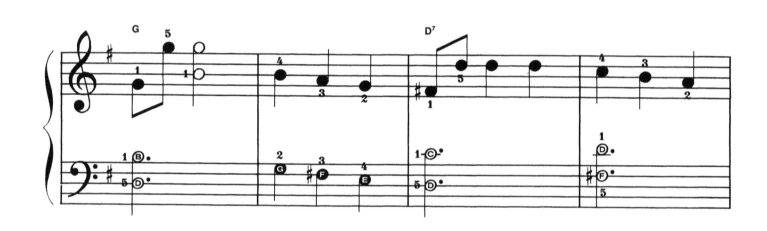

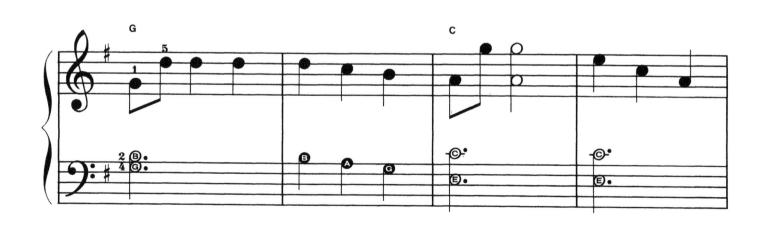

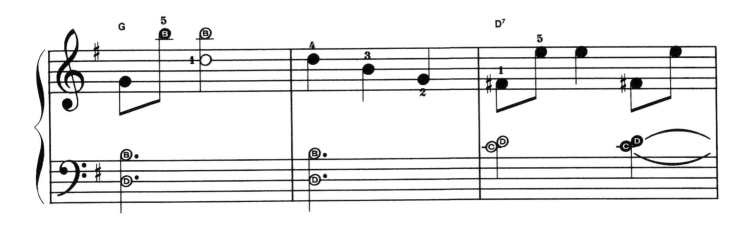

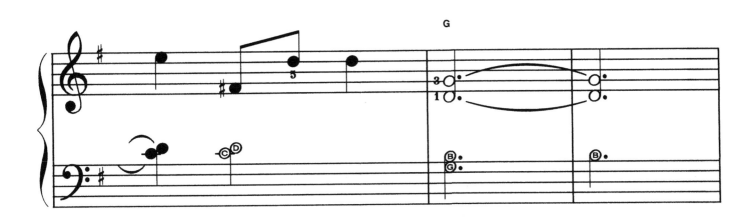

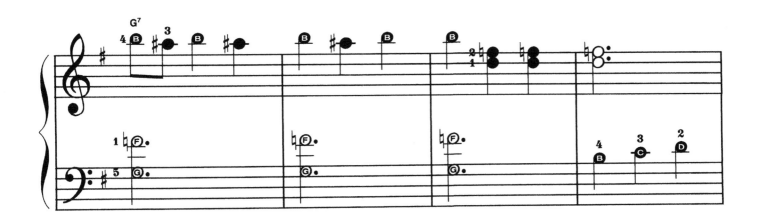

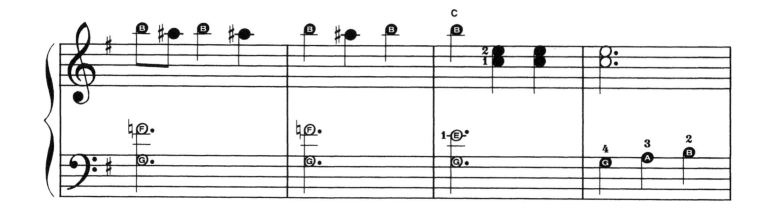

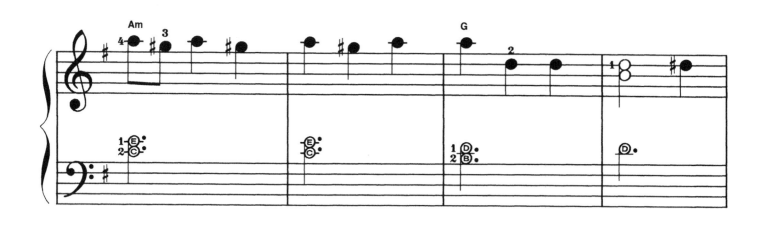

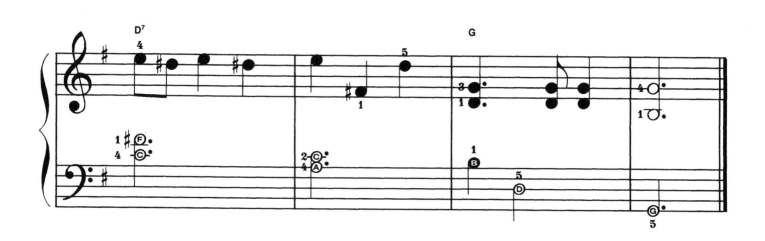

FUNERAL MARCH OF A MARIONETTE

CHARLES GOUNOD

Arranged by
JOE RAPOSO

SWAN LAKE

PETER I. TCHAIKOVSKY
Arranged by
JOE RAPOSO

Medium Slow

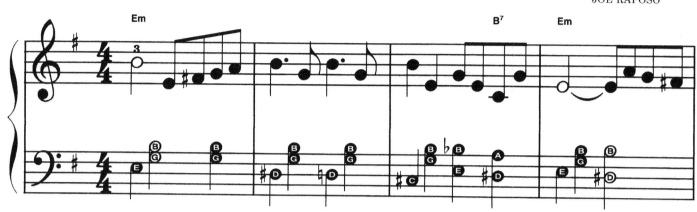

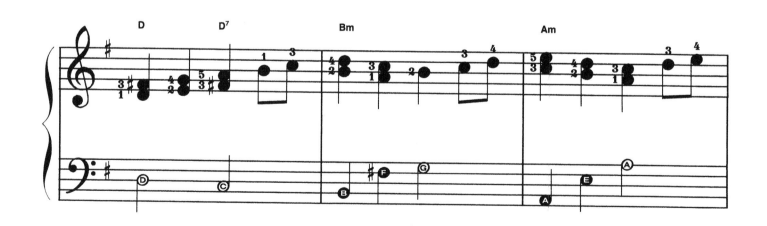

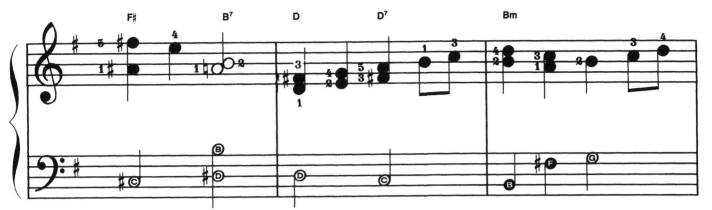
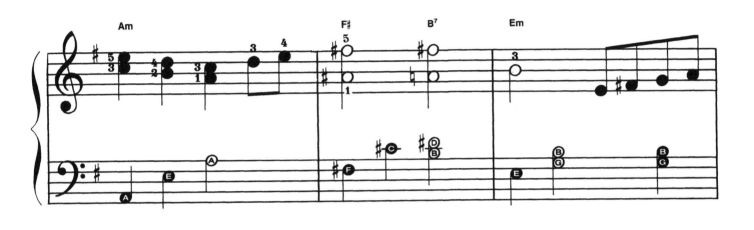
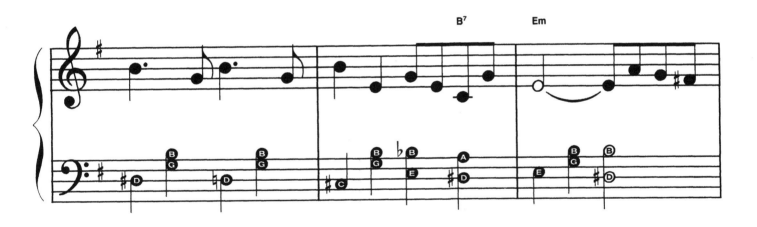

51

THE SWAN

CAMILLE SAINT-SAËNS

Arranged by
JOE RAPOSO

Medium Slow

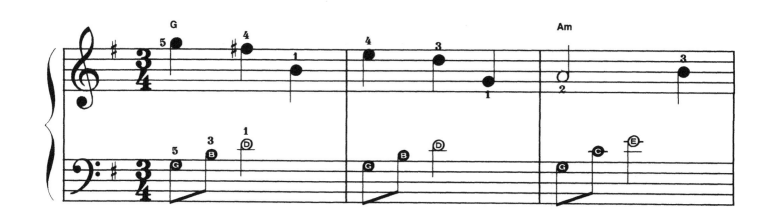

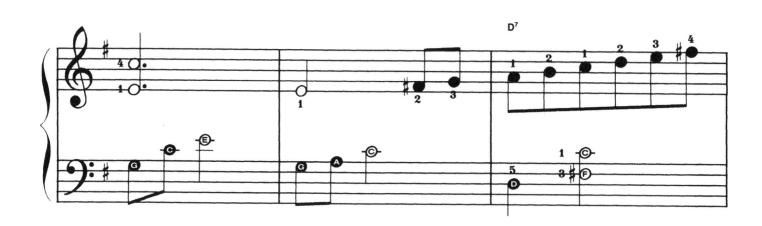

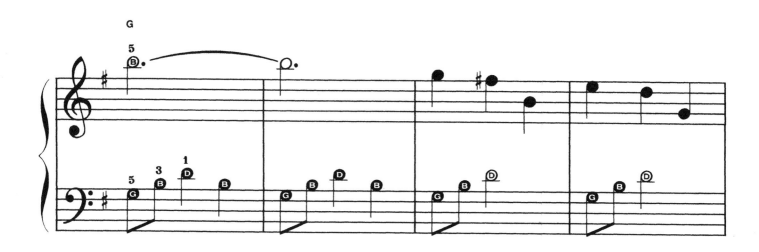

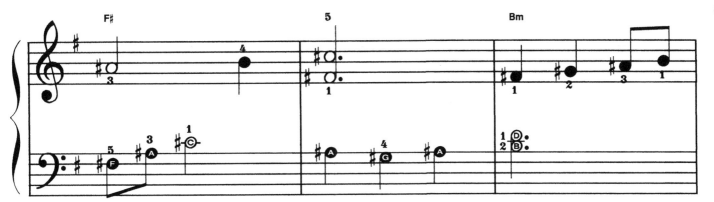

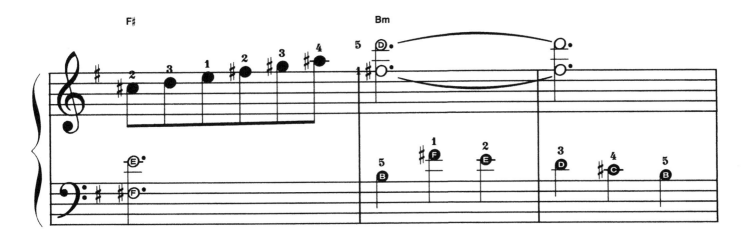

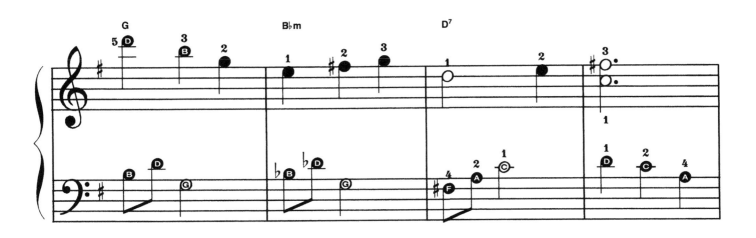

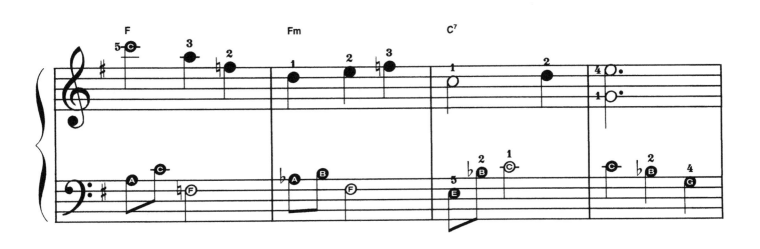

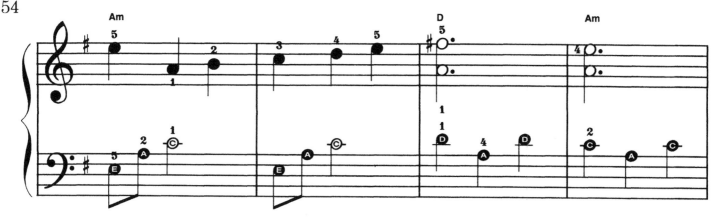

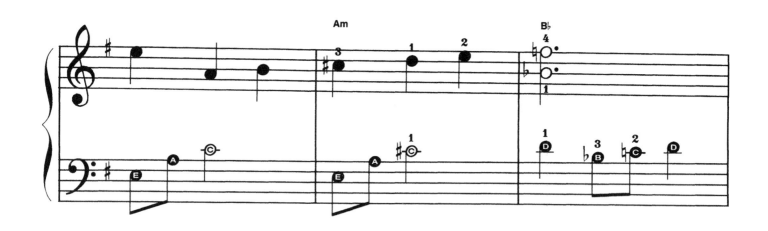

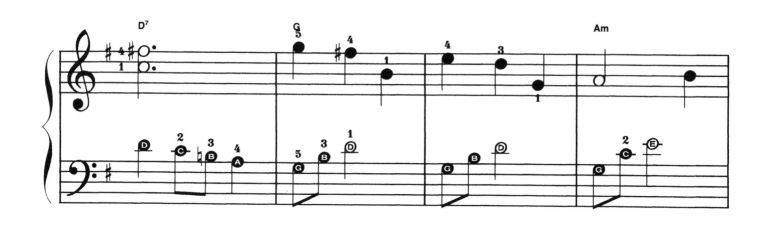

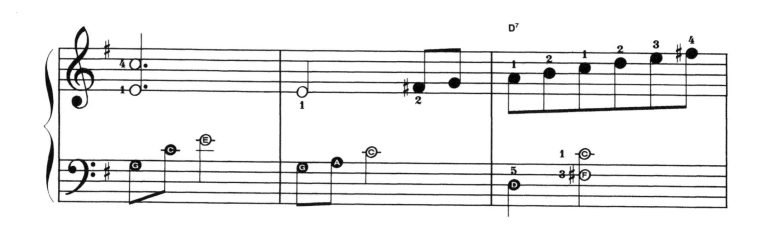

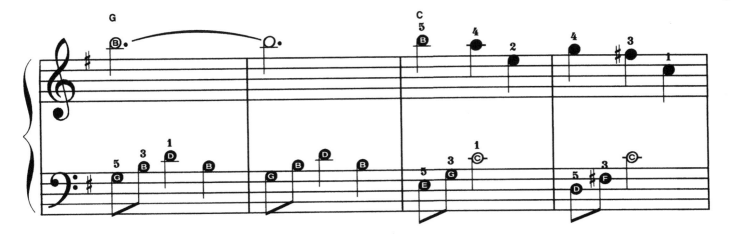

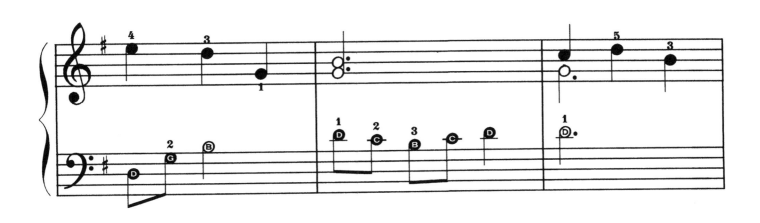

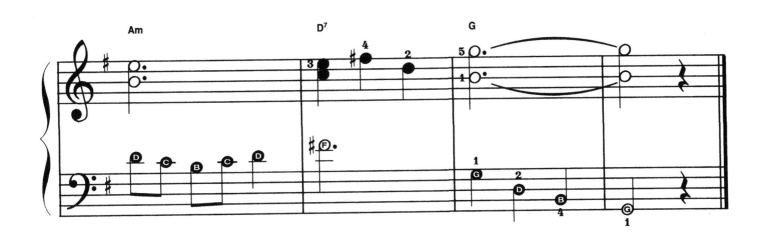

POLONAISE Op. 52

FREDERIC CHOPIN

Arranged by
JOE RAPOSO

Medium Fast

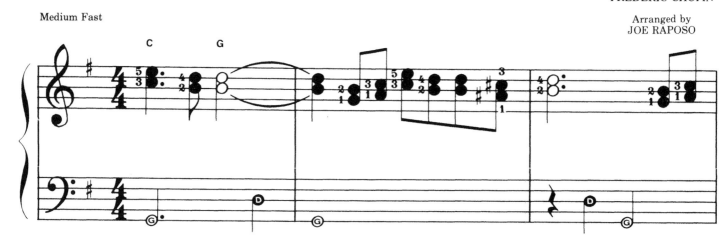

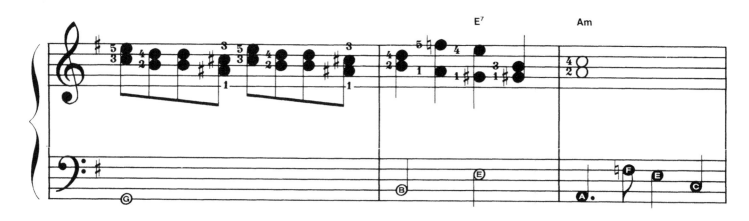

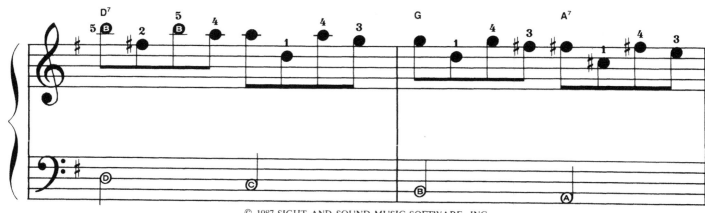

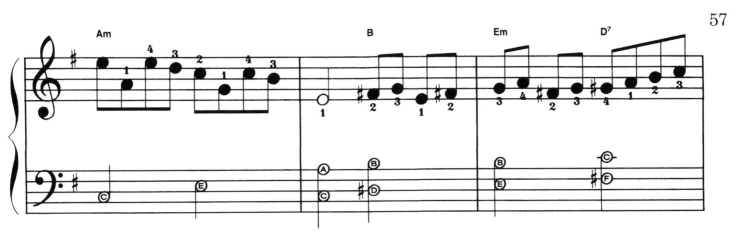

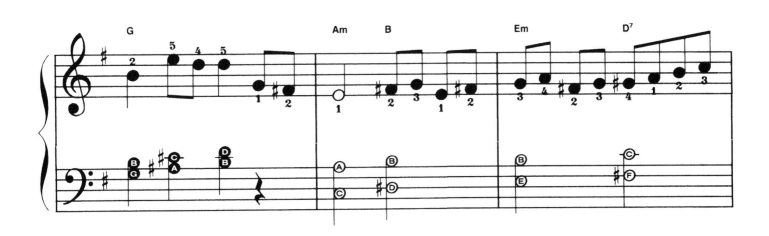

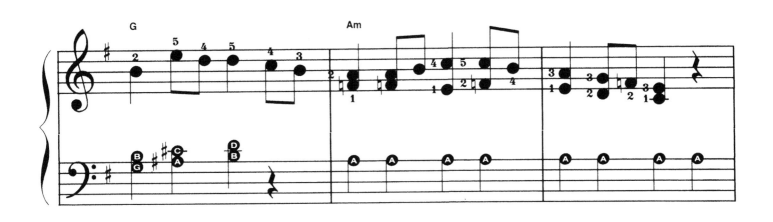

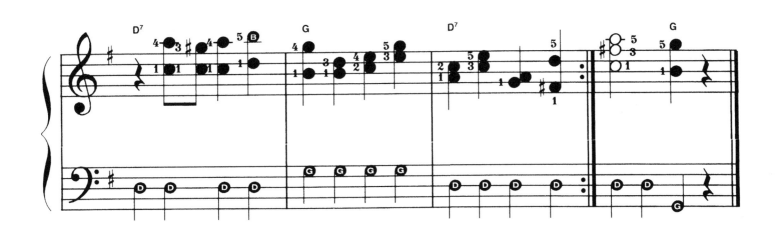

ROMEO AND JULIET

PETER I. TCHAIKOVSKY
Arranged by
JOE RAPOSO

Slow

59

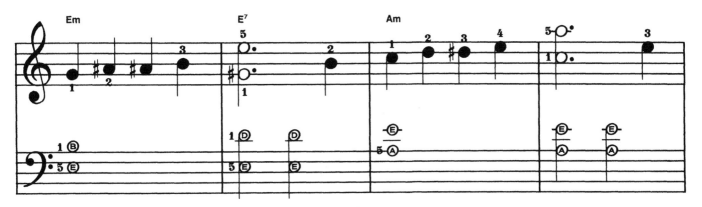

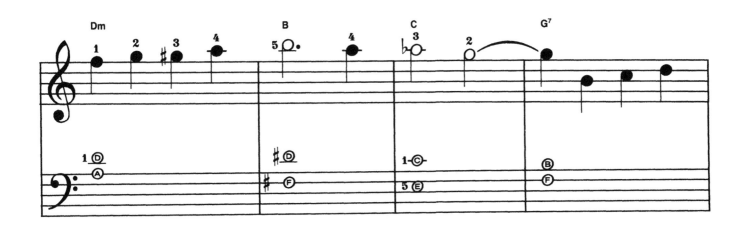

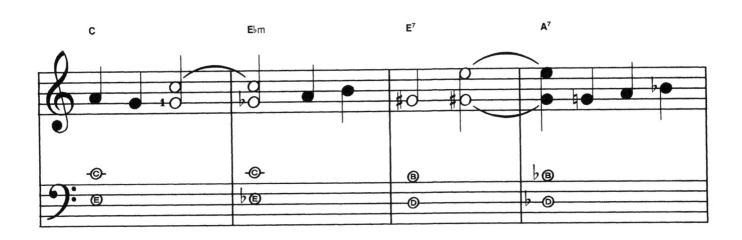

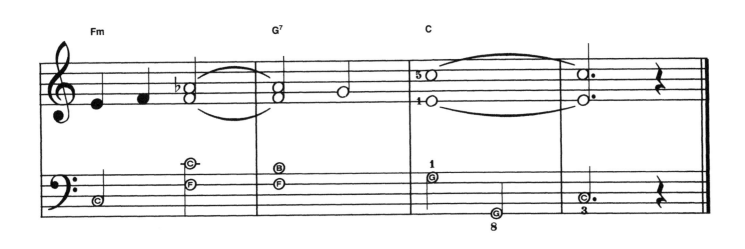

SLEEPING BEAUTY WALTZ

PETER I. TCHAIKOVSKY
Arranged by
JOE RAPOSO

Medium

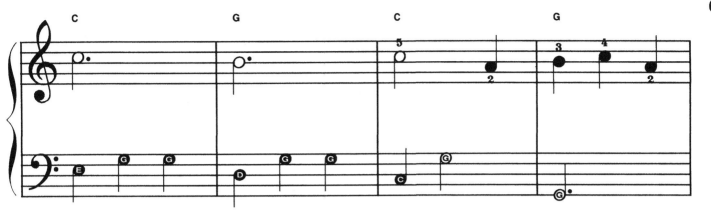

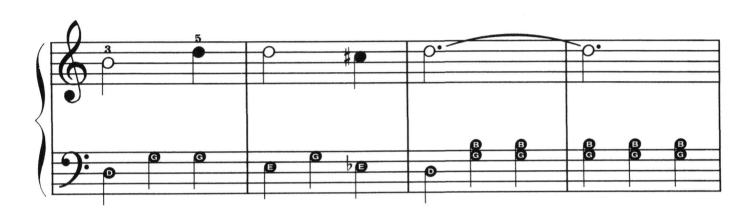

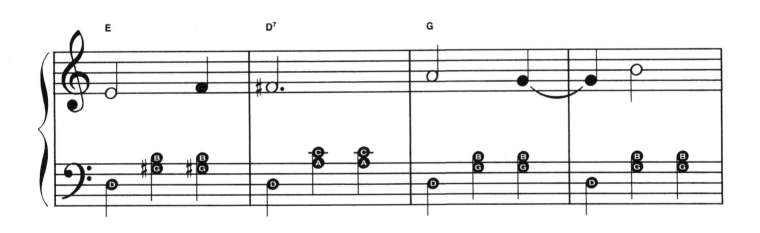

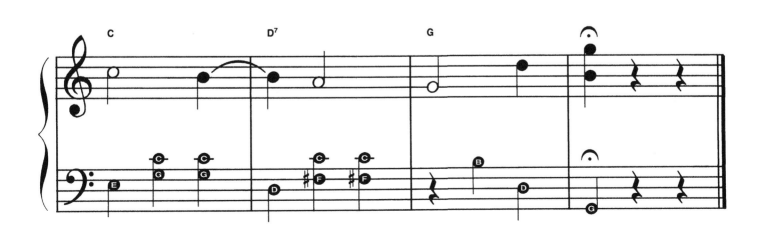

Hal Leonard Student Piano Library

Adult Piano Method

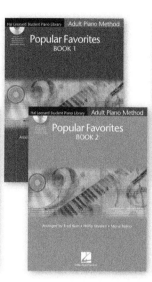

Adult Piano Method

Adults want to play rewarding music and enjoy their piano study. They deserve a method that lives up to those expectations. The *Hal Leonard Student Piano Library Adult Piano Method* does just that and more.

Method Book 1
00296441 Book/Online Audio $17.99

Method Book 2
00296480 Book/Online Audio $17.99

Popular Hits Book 1

Our hit-packed supplementary songbook includes these titles: American Pie • Circle of Life • Fun, Fun, Fun • Let It Be Me • Murder, She Wrote • The Music of the Night • My Heart Will Go On • Sing • Strangers in the Night • Vincent (Starry Starry Night) • Y.M.C.A. • The Way You Look Tonight.
00296541 Book/Online Audio $14.99

Popular Hits Book 2

12 hits: I Will Remember You • I Wish You Love • I Write the Songs • In the Mood • Moon River • Oh, Pretty Woman • The Phantom of the Opera • Stand by Me • Tears in Heaven • Unchained Melody • What a Wonderful World • When I'm Sixty-Four.
00296652 Book/Online Audio $14.99

Popular Favorites Book 1

11 favorites: Are You Lonesome Tonight? • Bless the Broken Road • Don't Know Why • Every Breath You Take • From a Distance • Help Me Make It Through the Night • I Hope You Dance • Imagine • Lean on Me • The Nearness of You • Right Here Waiting.
00296826 Book/Enhanced CD Pack.. $12.99

Popular Favorites Book 2

12 classics: All I Have to Do Is Dream • Georgia on My Mind • I Just Called to Say I Love You • I'm a Believer • Memory • Never on a Sunday • On My Own • One Fine Day • Satin Doll • That'll Be the Day • We Are the World • Your Song.
00296842 Book/Enhanced CD Pack.. $12.99

Christmas Favorites Book 1

12 favorites: Away in a Manger • Deck the Hall • God Rest Ye Merry, Gentlemen • I Saw Three Ships • Jingle Bells • Joy to the World • O Come, O Come, Emmanuel • O Little Town of Bethleham • Silent Night • Ukrainian Bell Carol • We Wish You a Merry Christmas • What Child Is This?
00296544 Book/Online Audio $14.99

Christmas Favorites Book 2

12 more holiday classics: Angels We Have Heard on High • Bring a Torch, Jeannette Isabella • Dance of the Sugar Plum Fairy • Ding Dong! Merrily on High! • The First Noel • Go, Tell It on the Mountain • Hark! The Herald Angels Sing • The Holly and the Ivy • O Christmas Tree • O Holy Night • Still, Still, Still • We Three Kings of Orient Are.
00296668 Book/Online Audio $14.99

Traditional Hymns Book 1

16 sacred favorites: All Glory, Laud and Honor • Come, Thou Almighty King • For the Beauty of the Earth • Holy, Holy, Holy! • It Is Well with My Soul • Joyful, Joyful, We Adore Thee • A Mighty Fortress Is Our God • What a Friend We Have in Jesus • and more.
00296782 Book/CD Pack..$12.99

Traditional Hymns Book 2

15 more traditional hymns: All Things Bright and Beautiful • Ezekiel Saw the Wheel • God of Grace and God of Glory • God Will Take Care of You • In the Garden • Lord, I Want to Be a Christian • Stand Up, Stand Up for Jesus • Swing Low, Sweet Chariot • This Is My Father's World • and more.
00296783 Book/CD Pack..$12.99

Prices, contents and availability are subject to change without notice.

www.halleonard.com